Small Sins

Published by Yowza Publishing
YowzaPublishing.com

ISBN: 978-1-951410-05-6

Version 1.0.0

Printing: 10 9 8 7 6 5 4 3 2 1

Scriptures are based on the World English Bible available online at: http://www.worldenglishbible.org/

Small Sins

Bradley Jones

This page intentionally blank

Chapter 1:

The Size of Sins

Most people believe there is a right and that there is a wrong. Many religions define things that are wrong as sins. The penalty for sins is often dependent upon the religious or moral path you follow. In some cases the impact of a sin is nothing. In other cases, if you don't turn from committing sins, you are facing an eternity in the burning flames.

Sins are a lot like dwarves. Many people focus on seven of them and ignore the rest.

The Seven Deadly Sins

Many people quickly acknowledge and often agree with the seven deadly sins. These are the sins that garner the most focus. It is not surprising that many people can name them:

- Lust
- Greed
- Envy
- Pride
- Sloth
- Gluttony
- Wrath

In today's society, some of these "deadly" sins have lost their potency. It is with pride that many Americans strive to gather the most money and possessions. People like Bill Gates and Warren Buffet are envied. Others strive hard to obtain similar riches. Envy and greed have become a part of societal expectations. The pride in which people show it is simply a matter of course.

Even so, many people still look at these as deadly sins that can lead to a person's downfall.

Commandments

In addition to deadly sends, there are the Christian commands that are also considered critical by many. There are those that believe that these Ten Commandments must also be followed in order to avoid falling into the category of sinner. These include:

- Not having other gods before you
- Not creating idols
- Not taking the Lord thy God's name in vain
- Not keeping the Sabbath day holy
- Not honoring your mother and father
- Not murdering
- Not committing adultery
- Not stealing
- Not bearing false witness
- Not coveting someone else's wife or other items

Like the deadly sins, several of the commandments are not held to the same levels today that they have in the past. For example, many people consider all seven days of the week equivalent. They don't recognize the Sabbath being a special day. Additionally, there is less focus on honoring parents.

In fact, there are some religions that don't hold these commandments at the same level as Christians. Pulling out a weapon and killing another person is nearly always considered a sin. It is nearly always, but not always. There are religious groups in the world that support the killing of "non believes." Additionally, many people tend to set aside their definition of murder when war is involved. Killing another person, specifically an enemy soldier, is often considered acceptable. Finally, a third example of killing that has many religious people overlooking the sinful aspects is capital punishment. If a person commits atrocious murder, then many consider the killing of that person justified. But is it? Is killing still a sin?

Varying Degrees

With murder the controversies tend to be limited. As you look at other sins listed in this book, they are sure to spur controversies as well. Hopefully the controversies will spur discussion. While many religions treat a sin as black or white, most people treat them as shades of grey. The more a sin can be treated in shades of grey, the more controversy is likely to arise.

The question that is rarely discussed is whether all sins are equal. Are each of the deadly sins is equal to the others? Does breaking a commandment about honoring your parents have the same penalty as stealing or murdering? Should the consequences be the same for showing pride at the same level as the person who murdered someone?

Will a person go to Hell or some similar bad place for sinning? If so, is a sin always punishable in this way? If this is the case, then it isn't the big sins that will get most people. Rather, it is the small sins.

This page intentionally blank

Chapter 2

The Small Sins

While some would consider the following to be venial sins that are relatively minor, each could be reasoned – or has been reasoned – to be a sin based on interpretations of the Holy Bible. In some cases, the sin being presented is derived as an example based on what is stated in a verse.

The verse that the sin is derived from is included on the page to the left. This provides a reference point for the sin.

You might find a few of the sins listed to be controversial, just as many religious philosophies and perspectives can be controversial. If you treat all the deadly sins as deadly, and if you believe the Ten Commandants must be followed, then you are likely to agree with the sins listed here. If you believe that the seven deadly sins and the Ten Commandments aren't relevant to today's society, then you are more likely to disagree with many of the sins listed in this book.

As you read through the list of sins, consider the following:

- How many of these do you believe are sins?
- How many of these have you committed?

"Thefts, covetousness, wickedness, deceit, lasciviousness, an evil eye, blasphemy, pride, foolishness: All these evil things come from within, and defile the man."

Mark 7:22-23

1

Arrogance

"A fool's lips enter into contention, and his mouth calleth for strokes. A fool's mouth is his destruction, and his lips are the snare of his soul."

Proverbs 18:6-7

2

Arguing

"An angry man stirreth up strife, and a furious man aboundeth in transgression."

Proverbs 29:22

3

Getting mad at your kids/parents

"Abstain from all appearance of evil"

1 Thessalonians 5:22

4

Playing Dungeons & Dragons

"I was a stranger, and ye took me not in: naked, and ye clothed me not: sick, and in prison, and ye visited me not. Then shall they also answer him, saying, Lord, when saw we thee an hungered, or athirst, or a stranger, or naked, or sick, or in prison, and did not minister unto thee? Then shall he answer them, saying, Verily I say unto you, Inasmuch as ye did it not to one of the least of these, ye did it not to me. And these shall go away into everlasting punishment: but the righteous into life eternal."

Matthew 25:43-46

5

Turning your back on – or not helping – the poor

"It is an honour for a man to cease from strife: but every fool will be meddling"

Proverbs 20:3

6

Meddling

"For I fear, lest by any means, when I come, I should find you not such as I would, and should myself be found of you such as ye would not; lest by any means there should be strife, jealousy, wraths, factions, backbitings, whisperings, swellings, tumults; lest again when I come my God should humble me before you, and I should mourn for many of them that have sinned heretofore, and repented not of the uncleanness and fornication and lasciviousness which they committed.

Corinthians 12:20-21

7

Gossiping

"I beseech you therefore, brethren, by the mercies of God, to present your bodies a living sacrifice, holy, acceptable to God, which is your spiritual service."

Roman 12:1

8

Getting a tattoo

"Therefore he who resists the authority, withstands the ordinance of God; and those who withstand will receive to themselves judgment."

Roman 13:2

9

Speeding
Driving 60 in a 55

There are six things which Yahweh hates;

yes, seven which are an abomination to him:

arrogant eyes, a lying tongue,

hands that shed innocent blood;

a heart that devises wicked schemes,

feet that are swift in running to mischief,

a false witness who utters lies,

and he who sows discord among brothers. "

Proverbs 6:16-19

10

Causing discord among others

"For I fear, lest, when I come, I shall not find you such as I would, and [that] I shall be found unto you such as ye would not: lest [there be] debates, envyings, wraths, strifes, backbitings, whisperings, swellings, tumults"

2 Corinthians 12:20

11

Envy

"But I say unto you, That whosoever is angry with his brother without a cause shall be in danger of the judgment: and whosoever shall say to his brother, Raca, shall be in danger of the council: but whosoever shall say, Thou fool, shall be in danger of hell fire."

Matthew 5:22

12

Getting angry at your brother or sister

"And lest thou lift up thine eyes unto heaven, and when thou seest the sun, and the moon, and the stars, even all the host of heaven, shouldest be driven to worship them, and serve them, which the LORD thy God hath divided unto all nations under the whole heaven."

Deuteronomy 4:19

13

Reading your horoscope

"O Timothy, keep that which is committed to thy trust, avoiding profane and vain babblings, and oppositions of science falsely so called"

1 Timothy 6:20

14

Speaking
Profanity

"Backbiters, haters of God, despiteful, proud, boasters, inventors of evil things, disobedient to parents, Without understanding, covenant breakers, without natural affection, implacable, unmerciful: Who knowing the judgment of God, that they which commit such things are worthy of death, not only do the same, but have pleasure in them that do them."

Romans 1:30:32

15

Boasting

"Wherefore they are no more twain, but one flesh. What therefore God hath joined together, let not man put asunder."

Matthew 19:6

16

Prompting someone to get a Divorce

"For when they speak great swelling words of vanity, they allure through the lusts of the flesh, through much wantonness, those that were clean escaped from them who live in error."

2 Peter 2:18

17

Vanity

"It hath been said, Whosoever shall put away his wife, let him give her a writing of divorcement: 32 But I say unto you, That whosoever shall put away his wife, saving for the cause of fornication, causeth her to commit adultery: and whosoever shall marry her that is divorced committeth adultery.

Matthew 5:31-32

18

Remarrying

"In like manner also, that women adorn themselves in modest apparel, with shamefacedness and sobriety; not with braided hair, or gold, or pearls, or costly array;"

1Timothy 2:9

19

Wearing an excessive amount of jewelry

"Seest thou a man *that is* hasty in his words? *there is* more hope of a fool than of him."

Proverbs 29:20

20

Speaking without thinking first

"*Whose mouth is full of cursing and bitterness: Their feet are swift to shed blood: Destruction and misery are in their ways: And the way of peace have they not known: There is no fear of God before their eyes.*"

Roman 3:14-18

21

Cursing

"Backbiters, haters of God, despiteful, proud, boasters, inventors of evil things, disobedient to parents, Without understanding, covenant breakers, without natural affection, implacable, unmerciful: Who knowing the judgment of God, that they which commit such things are worthy of death, not only do the same, but have pleasure in them that do them."

Romans 1:30:32

22

Not listening to your parents

"Owe no man anything, save to love one another: for he that loveth his neighbor hath fulfilled the law."

Romans 13:8

23

Using credit cards

"Therefore he who resists the authority, withstands the ordinance of God; and those who withstand will receive to themselves judgment."

Romans 13:2

24

Jaywalking

"The people were complaining in the ears of Yahweh. When Yahweh heard it, his anger was kindled; and Yahweh's fire burnt among them, and consumed some of the outskirts of the camp."

Numbers 11:1

25

Complaining

"I desire therefore that the men in every place pray, lifting up holy hands without anger and doubting."

Timothy 2:8

26

Doubting

" The overseer therefore must be without reproach, the husband of one wife, temperate, sensible, modest, hospitable, good at teaching; not a drinker, not violent, not greedy for money, but gentle, not quarrelsome, not covetous; "

1 Timothy 3:2

27

Drinking
(Being a drinker)

"But if that evil servant should say in his heart, 'My lord is delaying his coming,' 24:49 and begins to beat his fellow servants, and eat and drink with the drunkards, the lord of that servant will come in a day when he doesn't expect it, and in an hour when he doesn't know it,"

Matthew 24:49-50

28

Eating or drinking with drunks

"You masters, do the same things to them, and give up threatening, knowing that he who is both their Master and yours is in heaven, and there is no partiality with him."

Ephesians 6:9

29

Not treating employees right

"The overseer therefore must be without reproach, the husband of one wife, temperate, sensible, modest, hospitable, good at teaching; not a drinker, not violent, not greedy for money, but gentle, not quarrelsome, not covetous;"

1 Timothy 3:2

30

Being Greedy

"Behold, the Lord came with ten thousands of his holy ones, to execute judgment on all, and to convict all the ungodly of all their works of ungodliness which they have done in an ungodly way, and of all the hard things which ungodly sinners have spoken against him." These are murmurers and complainers, walking after their lusts (and their mouth speaks proud things), showing respect of persons to gain advantage."

Jude 14-15

31

Complaining

"*In the same way, that women also adorn themselves in decent clothing, with modesty and propriety; not just with braided hair, gold, pearls, or expensive clothing;*"

1 Timothy 2:9

32

Not dressing
modestly if you
are a woman

"Or know ye not that your body is a temple of the Holy Spirit which is in you, which ye have from God? and ye are not your own; for ye were bought with a price: glorify God therefore in your body"

1 Corinthians 6:19-20

33

Smoking

"For from within, out of the heart of men, evil thoughts proceed, fornications, thefts, murders, adulteries, covetings, wickednesses, deceit, lasciviousness, an evil eye, railing, pride, foolishness: all these evil things proceed from within, and defile the man"

Mark 7:21-23

34

Stealing

"*Verily I say unto thee, thou shalt by no means come out thence, till thou have paid the last farthing.*"

Mathew 5:26

35

Not paying off your credit cards on time

"The overseer therefore must be without reproach, the husband of one wife, temperate, sensible, modest, hospitable, good at teaching; not a drinker, not violent, not greedy for money, but gentle, not quarrelsome, not covetous;"

1 Timothy 3:2

36

Quarreling with others

"In the same way, that women also adorn themselves in decent clothing, with modesty and propriety; not just with braided hair, gold, pearls, or expensive clothing;"

1 Timothy 2:9

37

Wearing too much "bling" as a woman

"Backbiters, haters of God, despiteful, proud, boasters, inventors of evil things, disobedient to parents, Without understanding, covenant breakers, without natural affection, implacable, unmerciful: Who knowing the judgment of God, that they which commit such things are worthy of death, not only do the same, but have pleasure in them that do them."

Romans 1:30:32

38

Inventing evil things

"The overseer therefore must be without reproach, the husband of one wife, temperate, sensible, modest, hospitable, good at teaching; not a drinker, not violent, not greedy for money, but gentle, not quarrelsome, not covetous;"

1 Timothy 3:2

39

Not being hospitable

"Behold, the Lord came with ten thousands of his holy ones, to execute judgment on all, and to convict all the ungodly of all their works of ungodliness which they have done in an ungodly way, and of all the hard things which ungodly sinners have spoken against him." These are murmurers and complainers, walking after their lusts (and their mouth speaks proud things), showing respect of persons to gain advantage."

Jude 14-16

40

Lusting

"Yet in the same way, these also in their dreaming defile the flesh, despise authority, and slander celestial beings."

Jude 8

41

Having dirty dreams

"He said to them, "Beware! Keep yourself from covetousness, for a man's life doesn't consist of the abundance of the things which he possesses."

Luke 12:15

42

Gambling

"There are six things which Yahweh hates;

yes, seven which are an abomination to him:

arrogant eyes, a lying tongue,

hands that shed innocent blood;

a heart that devises wicked schemes,

feet that are swift in running to mischief,

a false witness who utters lies,

and he who sows discord among brothers."

Proverbs 6:16-19

43

Plotting to do something bad

"He shall not be afraid of evil tidings: his heart is fixed, trusting in the LORD."

Psalms 112:7

44

Being afraid of evil things or messages

"Owe no one anything, except to love one another; for he who loves his neighbor has fulfilled the law."

Romans 13:8

45

Having a home mortgage

Prologue

Do you have your own idea of a small sin? Feel free to email us at TheBook@SmallSins.com with the sin and the verse(s) you would use as a reference. While this book uses the Holy Bible for reference, feel free to use other religious documents as reference for any sins you'd like to submit.

www.ingramcontent.com/pod-product-compliance
Lightning Source LLC
Chambersburg PA
CBHW071819020426
42331CB00007B/1554